God at Work

*Cycle A Gospel Sermons for
Pentecost Sunday Through
Proper 12*

R. Kevin Mohr

CSS Publishing Company, Inc.
Lima, Ohio

GOD AT WORK
CYCLE A GOSPEL SERMONS FOR
PENTECOST SUNDAY THROUGH PROPER 12

FIRST EDITION
Copyright © 2016
by CSS Publishing Co., Inc.

Published by CSS Publishing Company, Inc., Lima, Ohio 45807. All rights reserved. No part of this publication may be reproduced in any manner whatsoever without the prior permission of the publisher, except in the case of brief quotations embodied in critical articles and reviews. Inquiries should be addressed to: CSS Publishing Company, Inc., Permissions Department, 5450 N. Dixie Highway, Lima, Ohio 45807.

Library of Congress Cataloging-in-Publication Data

Names: Mohr, R. Kevin, 1956- author.
Title: God at work : sermons for Cycle A Pentecost Sunday to Proper 12 / R. Kevin Mohr.
Description: FIRST EDITION. | Lima : CSS Publishing Company, 2016.
Identifiers: LCCN 2016024796 | ISBN 9780788028656 (alk. paper)
Subjects: LCSH: Bible. Gospels--Sermons. | Sermons, American--21st century. | Pentecost season--Sermons. | Church year sermons. | Common lectionary (1992). Year A.
Classification: LCC BS2555.54 .M64 2016 | DDC 252/.64--dc23
LC record available at https://lccn.loc.gov/2016024796

For more information about CSS Publishing Company resources, visit our website at www.csspub.com, email us at csr@csspub.com, or call (800) 241-4056.

e-book:
ISBN-13: 978-0-7880-28XX-X
ISBN-10: 0-7880-28XX-X

ISBN-13: 978-0-7880-2865-6
ISBN-10: 0-7880-2865-0

PRINTED IN USA

Table of Contents

Introduction	5

Pentecost Day 7
The Kiss of Life
John 20:19-23

Holy Trinity Sunday 11
Worship, Doubt, and the Trinity
Matthew 28:16-20

Proper 6 / Pentecost 2 / Ordinary Time 11 15
Good for What Ails Us
Matthew 9:35—10:8

Proper 7 / Pentecost 3 / Ordinary Time 12 21
Cross Choices
Matthew 10:24-39

Proper 8 / Pentecost 4 / Ordinary Time 13 27
Welcome, Inc.
Matthew 10:40-42

Proper 9 / Pentecost 5 / Ordinary Time 14 33
Prisoners of Hope
Matthew 11:16-19, 25-30

Proper 10 / Pentecost 6 / Ordinary Time 15 39
Lord, Let My Heart Be Good Soil
Matthew 13:1-9, 18-23

Proper 11 / Pentecost 7 / Ordinary Time 16 43
Dealing with T-A-R-E-ists
Matthew 13:24-30, 36-43

Proper 12 / Pentecost 8 / Ordinary Time 17
A Working God
Matthew 13:31-33, 44-52

Introduction

The lectionary gospel readings for the first third of the season after Pentecost (Pentecost Sunday through Proper 12) launch us immediately into a series of teachings by Jesus, many in the form of a parable, about what it means to follow him in the kingdom of God. Only three of the eight readings, for example, narrate distinct events in the ministry of Jesus. Given the heavy pedagogic emphasis in the other eight lections, it would be easy to treat discipleship as a thing or an object to be studied at a safe, intellectual distance. Nothing could be further from what I believe the Holy Spirit wants us to experience as we grapple with these readings. The parables and teachings of Jesus in Matthew, chapters seven through thirteen, illustrate what began at Pentecost: God is at work in the world through those who believe in Jesus Christ. As a theological "geek" my default tendency is to explain the things of God, rather than describe them. My prayer is that through these musings the reader might be able to catch enough of a glimpse of God at work to be caught up again into what God is doing in Christ Jesus through his church.

The sermons presented here are generally more topical or thematic than expository. All of them have been edited from their original context of sermons shared with the people of English Evangelical Lutheran Church in Bluffton, Ohio. My hope and prayer is that the liveliness and spirit of these messages has not been lost in the editing. It has been my great privilege and joy to wrestle with God's word with that great community of believers in Bluffton; I have been blessed to see God at work among them and through them. I am thankful to God for their role in these sermons — and to my wife, Deborah, who "gently" edited the messages the night before I originally preached them — but all of the weaknesses, mistakes, and — God forbid — unintended heresies are solely mine.

Pentecost Day
John 20:19-23

The Kiss of Life

The first kiss is a very powerful and meaningful thing, right?

Recently I read a report in a magazine stating that the average American claims to have had 26 first kisses. Wow! What that says to me is that I missed out on a lot of first kisses! My wife's take on that is not surprisingly, significantly different.

Don't spend the next fifteen minutes trying to remember, and then adding up, the number of your first kisses; let's try to stay focused folks.

Again, a kiss is a powerful thing. All the fairy tales know it: *Snow White, Sleeping Beauty, Cinderella*, and so on. But how does the Bible in general, and the story of Pentecost specifically, fit into this discussion about kissing? Some say the first kiss recorded in scripture comes right at the beginning, in Genesis 2. God breathed the breath of life into the first human, performing the first, primordial mouth to mouth resuscitation — which, by the way, is often known as the kiss of life. The gospel reading for today seems to echo or hark back to the creation story in Genesis. When Jesus promises the gift of the Holy Spirit, he then breathes on his disciples the breath of resurrection life.

My dad, who was a registered nurse, could always tell if one of us kids was sick simply by our breath. Right in the middle of some family activity, if my dad noticed that one of us four children was out of sorts, he would stop what he was doing and say to that child, "Breathe on me!" Then he would pronounce that my twin brother, or one of my two younger sisters, or I was coming down with a cold or an infection — and sure enough, he was invariably correct!

Now the gospel reading for this Pentecost Sunday isn't about bad, unhealthy breath, but the true, refreshing breath of life. Like the wonder of a first kiss, the true breath of life changes everything. It changes you and your outlook on life. Paradoxically, this spiritual kiss of life is based on the death of another — of our loved one — Jesus. In today's reading we go back into the Easter season and one of Jesus' earliest resurrection appearances. The risen Christ shows up unexpectedly in the upper room to confront the disciples' lingering fears and doubts with his blessing of peace, but they don't get it at first. They can't appreciate Jesus' appearance to them until they see the scars on his hands and in his side. Then, we are told, they rejoiced.

While the disciples didn't understand at first, interestingly, all the fairy tales seem to get it. True, most fairy tales end with everyone living "happily ever-after," but to get there the heroine and the hero always have to go through struggle and suffering and even sometimes a mortal wound before that transformative first kiss of true love. True love, in almost all of the best stories, is proved through suffering, which is a thoroughly biblical concept.

Therefore, the disciples were glad to see the scars of Jesus because, by seeing the wounds on his hands and in his side, they knew this wasn't just a dream or wishful thinking. This relationship with God through Jesus wasn't like a schoolkid crush or a one-night stand — the scars were proof that God was serious and committed and faithful, no matter what.

We need to see the scars. The scars prove that God has truly dealt with us and our root problem of sin and rebellion. It is the scars that prove the penalty for our sin has been paid, once and for all. The scars remind us of how precious we are in the sight of God. It is the scars that make it all real.

So the disciples then knew, and we can know now, that what God did in Christ Jesus was the real thing. The real one was standing before those trembling disciples, so that when Jesus breathed on them it was the true kiss of life they received. That "kiss" meant a new beginning, a new creation was breathed by God into existence, and that breath has been passed on down to us here today in this place.

The power of this ultimate kiss of life is the power of forgiveness: after he breathed on his disciples in the upper room, Jesus said to them:

> *Receive the Holy Spirit. If you forgive the sins of any, they are forgiven them; if you retain the sins of any, they are retained.*
> — John 20:22b-23

The gift of God's Spirit to God's people is not first and foremost about spectacular signs and wonders that we can now do, but about forgiveness: receiving it and giving it out. We are sent with the same mission as that upon which the Father sent the Son. The Spirit breathed into us is not a spirit of timidity, but one that opposes all evil and injustice, and dares to stand up to evil in defense of others, as Jesus did. However, our only weapon for battling the evil in us and around us is the power of the forgiveness of sins and the kiss of peace.

We breathe in God's forgiveness of us through the cross of Christ, and breathe out the blessing of God's peace through our pronouncement of God's forgiveness of others in Jesus' name. The kiss of God's Spirit working through forgiveness is the only thing that can revive stale relationships, and it has the power to breathe new, unexpected life into dead relationships. Again, forgiveness is actually the only power that we, as believers, have, but it is the most powerful force in the entire world. God's Spirit active in us is the spirit of forgiveness let loose on the world, so that the kiss of God's love can awaken the dead, free the enslaved, and open the hearts and minds of those who have been blinded by the power of sin, death, and the devil.

In other words, this new Spirit-filled life is not to be kept safely locked up behind closed doors of fear, doubt, and selfish self-righteous contentment with the status quo; we are sent out even as the Son was sent to us. Jesus could not be held down by the power of death in the tomb. Neither can we, who have had the life-giving power of the Holy Spirit breathed into us, stay behind closed doors for long. There are still doubting, hurting, lonely people out there whose fear and skepticism can be transformed into faith. There are people out there who need to be raised up from the death of despair, and whose hearts can be made glad by seeing the scars of the risen Christ through our lives of love and forgiveness.

It's time for us who have already been kissed by God's Spirit to give out the kiss of life through the forgiveness of sins to others. It's time to break the enchantment so that they too might live eternally ever after.

Amen.

Holy Trinity Sunday
Matthew 28:16-20

Worship, Doubt, and the Trinity

Worship, doubt, and the Trinity — strange bedfellows, right? The odd one out is obviously doubt, isn't it? Worship is one of the central activities of faith-filled people. The Trinity is an essential and distinguishing doctrine of the Christian faith. Clearly, the two go well together. But doubt? How did doubt creep in there, into this triumphant final scene after the resurrection when Jesus is saying goodbye to his disciples before ascending into heaven?

When they saw him, they worshiped him; but some doubted.
— Matthew 28:17

This doubt mixed in there with worship and the Trinity offends our sensibilities because we want things to be sure and certain, black and white. We want to get it right. That is especially true for someone like me, as a firstborn child, but we all probably suffer from the condition to some extent. We tend to project our obsessive-compulsive anxious nature onto God and how we relate to our Creator and others. We think we want a world governed by a strict binary function, like basic computer code: a one or a zero; either or; this or that; yes or no; you have or you have not; she loves me, she loves me not; you're in or you're out; you're a success or a failure; you believe or you don't believe.

But if that is how God relates to us and deals with us, then I guess it means we're all out, because who among us has never had any doubts about God and his relationship to us? Thank God — and I mean that literally — this binary function of "either this or that" is not how God works at all according to the gospel reading for this Trinity Sunday.

In our most prideful moments we are tempted to believe that if we had been there with Jesus on that mountaintop, then we wouldn't have fallen prey to the confusion and doubt that affected the disciples then. But not so fast! Living between heaven, earth, and hell is not so easy. On every Sunday in every place where we gather for a mountaintop experience with Jesus, it is very much a mixed-bag community of God's people who come together. Some are ready to worship. Some may be full of doubts. The mix changes from day to day and from Sunday to Sunday depending on what has happened during the intervening time. True, the hope is that in the course of the worship time together faith will win out over our doubts, but as we gather we are a real mélange.

This worship-doubt mishmash can't be solved as in the movies, with a sudden download of all the faith and gifts necessary so we are immediately transformed into super-saints who can perform miracles, as Neo did in the *Matrix* movies. No, as long as we are in this life doubt will always be lurking about in the shadows of our faith journey. The only way to deal with the shadow of doubt is to keep shining the light of the promise of Christ's powerful presence with us through trust.

Former President George H.W. Bush went skydiving a few years back on his ninetieth birthday! The success of that adventure did not depend on his strength or ability, but simply on his trust in his parachute. Similarly, the success of the adventure of obeying Jesus and going out on his mission to make disciples of all nations in the name of the Triune God does not depend on our strengths or abilities, but on our trust again in the promise of Christ's powerful presence with us, even in the face of our doubts.

Amazingly, our doubts are not a problem for God, as we see in the gospel reading. When Jesus sees his doubting disciples he doesn't pull back and hold off. He doesn't say, "Okay, you guys are obviously not yet ready for taking on my mission to the world; come back when you've got it all together!" Jesus didn't give up on them, in spite of their doubts, even after they had seen all of the evidence of his resurrection. And he doesn't give up on us either!

Hear these words of affirmation and promise from God's word attesting to God's desire to use us in his rescue mission of the world: No matter how spiritually dysfunctional we may feel at any given moment as individuals or as a congregation, the apostle Paul's words to the church at Corinth still apply, "Now you are the body of Christ and individually members of it" (1 Corinthians 12:27). In Christ we are a new creation (2 Corinthians 5:16); we are God's masterpieces, "created in Christ Jesus for good works" (Ephesians 2:10). Peter, who so often vacillated between bold faith and doubt-filled fears, wrote that we are "a chosen race, a royal priesthood, a holy nation, God's own people, in order that [we] may proclaim the mighty acts of him who called [us] out of darkness into his marvelous light" (1 Peter 2:9). This is all the work of the Triune God, whose grace is sufficient to deal with every fear that oppresses us, whose power is made perfect in our weaknesses — yes, even in our doubts!

The great commission of Matthew 28 shows that the Triune God does not hold back from us. Verb upon verb is piled up: go, disciple, baptize, teach, obey, and remember. The key is probably that last one: remember. The only way we ever overcome our doubts and fears is by remembering what is true and essential.

At a family reunion recently one of my nephews was teaching his young child how to swim in the pool. Whenever his son would begin to panic in the water, my nephew would tell him to start floating on his back; he needed to be reminded of his basic buoyancy and trust the water to hold him up.

The remembrance of the promise of Christ's powerful presence with us is what holds us up. That memory is the only adequate antidote to the doubts that would infect us. Because the risen Christ is with us, always, and because all authority has been given to him, we can dare to go and make disciples of all nations, baptizing them in the name of the Father, and of the Son, and of the Holy Spirit, teaching them Christ's way of life. That is our high calling, and there's no doubt about it!

Amen.

Some concepts adapted from: *Trinitarian Congregations* by David Lose, 2014. http://www.workingpreacher.org/craft.aspx?post=3254.
The *Lectionary Gospel:Matthew 28:16-20* by Scott Hoezee http://cep.calvin-seminary.edu/sermon-starters/trinity-sunday-a/?type=the_lectionary_gospel.

Proper 6 / Pentecost 2 / Ordinary Time 11
Matthew 9:35—10:8

Good for What Ails Us

Before modern medical science really took off in the last fifty years of the past millennium, there were a lot of home and folk remedies being prescribed by well-meaning individuals, but also by con artists and charlatans. The remedy was often administered accompanied by the phrase that the supposed cure was "good for what ails you." The classic, all-purpose remedy for nearly every condition was a tablespoonful of castor oil. Perhaps some of you suffered through that treatment or gave it to someone else.

After settling on the title for this sermon, I "googled" the phrase "good for what ails you" on the internet. My search resulted in quite an interesting list of old and new products and activities that were or are supposedly good for what ails us. There were a couple of sites online that promoted humor as a good remedy for just about anything bad. Another site featured a jazz song with the lyric, "love is good for anything that ails you." It's hard to argue with that one!

According to the world wide web, Siberian ginseng and Yemeni honey are really good for you, as well as massage therapy, owning a pet, and aromatherapy. My favorite, though, among all of the old creams, salves, and liniments used a century ago was this one: Brame's Pain Knocker. The ingredients? 1.5% tincture of opium, 1.5% chloroform, and a whopping 88% alcohol content! Wow! Now there's a cure for what ails you!

Seriously, what does ail us? What ails the world?

The gospel reading tells us Jesus went out to the towns and villages, teaching, preaching, and healing every kind of disease and sickness. But beyond the physical ailments he also noticed that the crowds were harassed, confused, and helpless, like sheep without a shepherd. An aggressive predator can leave a flock of sheep either quivering and prostrate, paralyzed with fear or scattered, running helter-skelter, crazed with panic. Scripture tells us that we are, in fact, being stalked and attacked in this life by the predator of all predators — the devil, who is compared to a roaring lion, sneaking and prowling around to find someone to attack and devour (1 Peter 5:8).

Harassed, helpless, and confused: sounds like symptoms that fit our time and world, don't they? So many people feel harassed and helpless, locked into jobs and schedules that enslave and control rather than bring satisfaction and contentment. The *dis*-ease we experience at work or in our mismanagement of time then affects negatively all of our most important relationships, including the relationship with God. And when that happens, the devil roars with delight.

In this post-modern world where everything is presented as being relative, where all values are neutral, and where no absolute truth can supposedly be known with any certainty, confusion and instability reign supreme. We run helter-skelter, looking for a quick fix from one self-help guru with a new, *old* idea, to the next. But we never find lasting peace and wholeness and a solid place upon which to build our lives and our future. Satan sees it all and purrs with contentment at our confusion.

Everywhere we turn we are confronted with a society and lives full of physical, emotional, social, and spiritual sickness. How do we respond? What effect does the crowd have on us? Does its frenzied panic suck us in? Does its weary resignation fill us with fear or loathing? Or does the sight of the crowd, harassed and helpless like sheep without a shepherd, fill us with compassion, as it did Jesus?

Let's be clear about this: Jesus wasn't just "sorry" for the crowd, as one translation has it. No, the Greek word used here in verse 36 — *splangnistheis* — means that Jesus was filled with a gut-wrenching compassion, a compassion that reached out in words and deeds. This gut-wrenching compassion would lead Jesus to the cross to die for the crowd, for the world, for you, for me, while we were yet helpless and harassed, confused and lost enemies of God.

Jesus came with the remedy for what ails the world — the good news of the reign of God's love, come to earth in him. The love of God has broken into our world in a radically new and paradoxically powerful way, bringing life, health, wholeness, and cleansing through the forgiveness of sins. Part of the paradox of the good news is that Jesus' followers — formerly harassed and panicked sheep without a shepherd themselves — are integral to God's remedy. We who have been marked with the cross of Christ forever in the waters of baptism, are claimed, gathered, and sent by God's goodness for the sake of the world because "the harvest is plentiful, but the laborers are few" (Matthew 9:37b).

The harvest is indeed plentiful. For example, on the rolls of the congregation I currently serve, we list over 300 members, but only about 120 actually worship with us in the course of a month. Are the other 180 or so out there harassed and helpless and possibly confused, trying to face life on their own, like sheep without a shepherd? The compassion of Christ compels us to reach out to them and, perhaps, be the means by which God's Spirit leads them back into the fold. Maybe it's the same in your congregation.

The harvest is plentiful. Again, the statistics for the two counties surrounding the congregation I currently serve show that 50% of the residents have no formal relationship to a Christian community. Perhaps it is the same where you live. If so, then we can't explain the lack of growth in our congregations by mouthing any nonsense about everyone being a Christian in our area! There are harassed and helpless people out there, around the corner from where we live, working in the same factory, in the next cubicle to ours, living across the street, right next door — perhaps even in the same house with us. They are lost sheep without a shepherd, ready to respond to the good news.

Who is caring for them? Who will have compassion on them? The harvest *is* plentiful — it is the laborers who are few. That is why Jesus told his disciples then and tells us today to pray to the Lord of the harvest to send out laborers to bring in the harvest. Prayer is the first step; it is not a substitute for work, but the work will not be done without prayer. So we pray and work.

Notice, immediately after Jesus tells his disciples to pray that God would send out laborers into the harvest, he sends those whom he asked to pray out as the answer to that prayer. The principle at work here is what the reformer Martin Luther taught in his explanation of the Lord's Prayer: whenever we pray that God would do something, we first of all pray that God would begin with us.[1] We are Christ's hands and feet, now, today, in our world. We are part of God's answer to the prayer for laborers to bring in the harvest. The one who prays, does what God wants done, and the one who prays is ready to go where the need is and where God sends.

There's simply no escaping it: like the disciples before us, we are an integral part of God's remedy for what ails the world. Ordinary people like you and me are called by God for his extraordinary work in the world. Jesus' ministry is also ours: to do no harm, but to embody in our words and actions and attitudes God's remedy that is good for what ails the world. Where there is brokenness, we will bring reconciliation through the amazing power of the forgiveness of sins, revealed at the cross of Christ. When people feel excluded and ostracized, we will bring the cleansing touch of inclusion and welcome in Jesus' name. Where life is overshadowed by the fear of death, we will bring hope by proclaiming Christ's resurrection.

Wherever we find evil at work, whether at home, in the church, at school, at work, in society in general or whether half-way around the globe, we will oppose it with all our might in Jesus' name. His gut-wrenching compassion compels us so that others may be freed from bondage to falsehood and injustice. The compassion of the Triune God compels us so that the harassed and helpless of this world might come to know Jesus as we have come to know him: God's very personal remedy for what ails the world.

Amen.

---

1. See the *Small Catechism* by Martin Luther, online at http://bookofconcord.org/smallcatechism.php#lordsprayer 2008, accessed June 15, 2015

Proper 7 / Pentecost 3 / Ordinary Time 12
Matthew 10:24-39

Cross Choices

A man once told his friends of a system he had invented to preserve domestic peace. "The day we married ten years ago," he said, "we decided that all important decisions should be made by me. Small decisions were left to my wife." When his friends asked him how it had worked out, he replied, "Perfectly, there hasn't been a single hitch in the entire ten years. Of course," he added, "no important decision has come up yet."

The challenge of human existence is that life is made up of decisions, insignificant or crucial, mundane or complex. As we know from history and our own experiences, even the most trivial decision can have a huge impact on our lives and that of others. Therefore, it isn't always easy for us to make decisions.

That was especially true in our household when our two daughters were still at home. Let me explain: In the 1980s and 1990s there were a lot of studies being done on a unique group of people known as TCKs — third culture kids. TCKs are persons who have spent a significant part of their formative years growing up in another country and culture significantly different from that of their parents' country and culture of origin. One of the common traits of TCKs is that even as adults they have trouble making essentially unimportant everyday decisions in a group setting. Well, in a household with four missionary TCKs under one roof (our daughters were born in Madagascar, and both my wife and I grew up in Ethiopia and Papua, New Guinea, respectively), you can imagine how difficult it was for us to decide on which fast-food restaurant to eat at, or which video to rent!

On the other end of the spectrum, our modern world tends to minimize the importance of all decisions and choices, based on the widespread belief that there are no absolute "either/or" situations out there. We want it both ways, and naively hope that evil will somehow turn into good so that we don't have to be called on to make a final and total rejection of whatever it is we want to keep holding onto. But Christian apologist C.S. Lewis pointed out that this belief leads only to disaster because life is not like the radii of a circle, all leading eventually to the center, or even like tributary creeks and streams, all flowing together into the main river. No, Lewis argued that life as we experience it is far more like a road that continuously forks into new roads, or a tree whose branches keep spreading further and further apart. Another example of this principle is what we see in the breeding of dogs for specialization: "Good, as it ripens," Lewis wrote, "becomes continuously more different not only from evil but from other good."[1]

So the rescue of those who choose wrong roads in this life consists first, in stopping, and then in getting off the wrong road and getting onto the right one. Math errors, for example, simply don't go away from a calculation; you have to go back to the beginning and start all over. Error and evil can be undone, but time alone does not heal them, and they do not "evolve" or develop into good.

Life very rarely if ever presents us with "both/and" situations when it comes to important matters. Significant choices are almost always "either/or" situations. And that is never more true than when it comes to matters of ultimate concern. Jesus makes that clear in the gospel reading for today in the juxtaposition of love for parents or children and love for him. This extreme example, using the case of something that is in essence good — love for our relatives — highlights the radical nature of choosing discipleship and the way of God. Our choices reveal who we really are.

We see that truth revealed in the biblical witness from the very beginning. The first three chapters of the Bible lay out the foundation for understanding who we are and that for which we were created: We were created in the image of God as moral agents of decision, and our choices have consequences because we are of consequence in God's plan for the world. Decisions have to be made. We have to choose. But because there is potentially so much at stake, those choices aren't always easy for us. Whatever else the story of the fall in Genesis 3 teaches us, it clearly demonstrates that decisions and choices either move us away from or toward God.

The cost of discipleship is only really known then when we face situations requiring a decision. When we are confronted with crises, tests, and temptations that demand a choice — that is when the rubber hits the road. We recognize and realize the cost of discipleship at the crossroad and on the frontier as we journey with Jesus across boundaries. In those decisions we either do life and choose God's way, following Jesus, or we do death and choose poorly.

Scripture is full of stories of those kinds of choices. Moses in his farewell sermon, for instance, set before the children of Israel either the blessing of obedience to God or the curse of disobedience, calling on the people to choose life through obedience. Joshua, Moses' successor, would later ask the people to choose whom they would serve: the true God or the gods of their ancestors, "but as for me and my house," he concluded, "we will serve the Lord" (Joshua 24:15). Ruth, a young, destitute Moabite widow, had the reasonable opportunity to return to her family and the faith of her ancestors, but instead, she made her choice for the living God, saying to Naomi, her Jewish mother-in-law, "Where you go, I will go; ... your people shall be my people, and your God my God" (Ruth 1:16). As the result of her faithful decision, Ruth became the great grandmother of King David, and the ancestor of Jesus, the Messiah.

A thousand years later, a descendant of Ruth was faced with the angel's shocking announcement that would put her future at risk and completely change her life and that of human history. Even so, Mary responded saying, "Here am I, the servant of the Lord; let it be with me according to your word" (Luke 1:38). Thirty years afterward, Mary's son, Jesus, would ask his disciples first, "who do you say that I am?" and then, after some were deserting Jesus because of his message, he would then ask them, "Do you also wish to go away?" Peter answered for the disciples both times, saying, "You are the Christ, the Son of the living God," and "Lord, to whom can we go? You have the words of eternal life."

There is a choice to be made: the Buddha does not have the words of eternal life. Neither did Mohammed. The words of eternal life are not some cosmic force locked within you and me waiting to be released by self-actualization, or by the wisdom of some best-selling self-help book or guru. The words of eternal life that only Jesus has and offers are not based on self-help at all, but on its opposite: self-denial and the death of our selfish wills.

As Dietrich Bonhoeffer, the Lutheran martyr who died at the hands of Nazi Germany, said, "When Christ calls a person, he bids that person 'come and die.'"[2] Those words reflect what Jesus teaches us in verses 38-39 in the gospel reading as the crux of the matter: that taking up the cross and following Jesus means giving up self for Jesus' sake in order to find real life in him.

Only the person who is dead to his or her own selfish will can follow Christ. To choose life through the death of self and our affections, lusts, desires, wants, and allegiances is never easy. Every day we will encounter new temptations, and every day we ask God's Spirit to help us choose again to die to self and take up the cross. Again, the choice of the cross isn't easy — it wasn't for Jesus, as his anguish in the Garden of Gethsemane proves — but the choice of the cross was and is the right choice, the best choice. That it happens at all has nothing to do with our strength of character or innate abilities. That any of us manages to follow Jesus faithfully for even one minute, let alone for a lifetime, is truly a miracle of God's grace!

God's grace works its miracle on us, in us, and through us when, through prayer and praise and Bible study together with other believers, when we fix our eyes on Jesus, the pioneer and perfector of our faith. God's Spirit is the one who makes us fit to be Jesus' disciples in the world, willing and able to share with others how to find life by, paradoxically, giving it up for Jesus. To choose the cross of Christ is the best choice of all. You will never regret it!

Amen.

---

1. C.S. Lewis, *The Great Divorce* (New York:Macmillan, 1959), p. 128.
2. Dietrich Bonhoeffer, *The Cost of Discipleship* (London: SCM Press, 1948/2001), p. 44. Additional concepts from pp. 41-78, 86-93.

Proper 8 / Pentecost 4 / Ordinary Time 13
Matthew 10:40-42

Welcome, Inc.

The lady of the house was giving last minute instructions to her butler before the start of a huge dinner being held at the estate: "Bentley," she said, "I want you to stand at the front door and call the guests' names as they arrive." "Very well, madam," replied the butler, "I've been wanting to do that for years."[1]

One of the occupational hazards of being a butler is that you have to be welcoming to people who aren't particularly welcome-able. Actually, it isn't just butlers who have that experience. Waiters and waitresses, for example, have to put up with patrons who aren't always very pleasant or exactly welcome-able. I know this from experience, not because I've worked as a waiter, but because I am ashamed to admit I have been one of those grumpy customers!

Mormon missionaries and Jehovah's Witnesses are, in contrast, usually polite and pleasant. Still, few of us are thrilled when they, or any evangelists, come knocking, as we hear in the following story:

Two church members were going door to door. They knocked on the door of a home where the woman who opened it was not happy to see them. She told them in no uncertain terms that she did not want to hear their message and slammed the door in their faces. To her surprise, however, the door did not close. In fact, it bounced back open. She tried slamming the door again, really putting her back into it. The result was the same — the door bounced back open. Convinced that the unwanted callers must be sticking a foot in the doorway, she reared back to give it a slam that would teach them a lesson, when one of them said, "Ma'am, before you do that again, you need to move your cat out of the way."[2]

While it is true that door-to-door salespeople are getting rarer and rarer these days, they do have modern descendants. Telemarketers, computer spam, and pop-up window advertising are some of the unwelcome curses of the digital age.

Being welcoming and being welcome-able. As important as those characteristics are in sales, they are even more fundamental to what the kingdom of God is all about. Through Jesus Christ we get welcomed into the family of God; we are incorporated into — made a part of — what we could call "Welcome, Incorporated" or "Welcome, Inc.," the Body of Christ. The baptismal font is the ritual welcoming place where God formally and publicly welcomes us and claims us as his own and begins making us into followers of Jesus Christ.

As baptized followers of Jesus, his mission becomes ours: to proclaim the good news that God is in the business of welcoming the lost, the outcast, the forgotten, the stranger, even the enemy. When that message is incorporated into our lives and we give flesh and blood to that message, we become both welcoming of and welcome-able by others because of and through the power of the good news we bear.

We can be welcoming and welcome-able: because of the free gift of God: eternal life. Since the life God offers *is* a gift, we are not in competition with others for it, and because the life we are given in Christ is God's, it is not a non-renewable commodity or resource that will eventually run out, like oil. Beyond that, its price will not go up on us tomorrow or ever, because it was paid once and for all on the cross by God's own Son. Therefore, it is available to any and all who will receive it in faith.

But for that to happen, we who incorporate the message must be both welcoming and welcome-able, not just in words and theory but also in attitude and action. The Body of Christ — Welcome, Inc. — is to be full of open doors, open hearts, and open minds. Sometimes that is difficult for us because we are afraid; we see the world changing so much around us that we feel more and more like fish out of water. We begin to wonder if anyone will ever respond to the message we have to share. The good news for us is that in spite of the seriousness of discipleship as described in the verses immediately before the gospel reading for today, Jesus assures us some people will respond. They will respond if they can see Jesus at work in and through us, being welcoming of even the smallest of gestures of reception from others.

Does that mean anything goes, that we should compromise on just about everything in order to get people in the doors and make them feel welcome? Do we just cover up the dirt and the hard things? Well, that's not what Jeremiah, the prophet, did. He would not compromise on the truth of what God was saying when others were mouthing only what was politically correct at the time. (See Jeremiah 28:5-9.) He would not be a hypocrite and just cover up the dirt and tell people what they wanted to hear. Being incorporated into God's people does not mean business as usual. Being welcomed by God and becoming welcome-able to others results in changed lives.

The apostle Paul makes that clear in Romans 6. The most authentic witness to the good news of God's love occurs when, according to Paul, we present ourselves to God and no longer continue to habitually live in sin. In other words, through faith in what God has done for us in the life, death, and resurrection of Jesus Christ, we are set free from the power of sin to control our lives. Furthermore, we are enabled to please God and actually turn away from sinful behaviors and attitudes that hurt us and others and our relationship to God.

On the other hand, there is nothing more damaging to our witness than when others can label us as hypocrites because we try to present ourselves as "holier-than-thou" "super-Christians" who never stumble. That simply isn't reality. The bumper sticker I have on display in my office expresses the true situation: "Christians aren't perfect, just forgiven." Always remembering that we are forgiven sinner-saints is the proper welcoming and welcome-able attitude to have. It is the attitude that brings welcome relief and allows others to respond to Jesus Christ and become part of Welcome, Inc. — to become incorporated into God's kingdom.

Many of our Christian social service agencies are good models for this welcoming and welcome-able attitude. One such agency in the region where I currently minister is the Wernle Youth and Family Treatment Center in Richmond, Indiana. Wernle is a welcoming place for the forgotten, the rejected, those upon whom society has, perhaps, given up, those who have been hurt and those who have hurt others. The center does that by providing opportunities for growth and development of troubled children and their families through caring programs and healing relationships that are reflective of God's love revealed in Jesus Christ.[3]

Isn't that a good summary of what we are to be about as a community of believers? Shouldn't we be caring people in a caring community embodying healing relationships that are reflective of God's love revealed in Jesus Christ? What a responsibility and privilege! God has decided on the route of incarnation and incorporation — and no other route. In other words, God dares to entrust us with his message of welcome completely, so completely, in fact, that we are invited and challenged to actually take the message into us and, in a certain sense, become the message. When that happens, we become welcoming to and welcome-able by others so that,

they too can have access to God's free gift — eternal life. It is our mission to share that life with others. At this and every branch of Welcome, Inc. sharing the welcoming good news of Jesus Christ is our business, our only business.
Amen.

Some concepts from *No Small Gestures*, by David Lose, 2014, at http://www.workingpreacher.org/craft.aspx?post=3265
1. Found at http://workjokes.tripod.com/more_a/butler_2.html
2. Found at http://www.answerology.com/index.aspx/question/3084724_Two-church-members-were-going-door-to-door-.html
3. See www.wernle.org for information on Wernle. The center is affiliated with Lutheran Services in America.

Proper 9 / Pentecost 5 / Ordinary Time 14
Matthew 11:16-19, 25-30

Prisoners of Hope

We humans are really good at excuses. We've had lots of practice since Adam and Eve started the ball rolling by first blaming each other, then the serpent, and finally even blaming God for their rebellion against their Creator. Give us enough time and we can justify or rationalize away just about anything we do, especially when it comes to our relationship with God. Let me give you a true-life example.

A number of years ago, our family went white water rafting down the New River in West Virginia. At one point on the trip our guide (let's call her "Heather") was alone in the raft with me while my wife and our two daughters were swimming in a calm stretch of the river. Heather did what people often seem to feel compelled to do when confronted with a pastor: she launched into a half-confession, and then tried to back-peddle (or, I should say, since we were rafting, back-paddle) out of it. Heather admitted she didn't go to church much anymore, even though her mother was trying to encourage her to do so, especially now that she had a young daughter. That's when Heather began to back-*paddle* and attempted to rationalize away her behavior. She tried to get me to agree with her that the beauty of the New River gorge was her church, and couldn't she commune with God just as well out on the river as in any building with a bunch of people? I gently and humorously told Heather that I thought her mother was a pretty wise person in this case.

Excuses, self-justification, and rationalization — we've all done it at different times in different ways! Some of us justify our low level of giving for God's work, for example, by blaming the national headquarters of our denomination for being too liberal; others quit participating in Sunday school or Bible studies because the rest of the members or the pastor are too conservative. God convicts us of a particular sin in our life and of the need for change, and we immediately come up with all kinds of excuses, blaming our weakness either on our genes or on our upbringing or on both nature and nurture. Or we try to rationalize it all away:

> "Hey, I admit I'm not perfect as a husband, but no marriage is perfect, right?"
> "Okay, I'm no saint, but I'm just as good as the next person!"
> "Everybody else is doing it, why shouldn't I?"
> "I've got too much on my plate right now. I'll get to that soon, God, maybe next week!"

All of our excuses, however, are just a smokescreen to help cover up the weariness we feel, and to hide the heavy mess of our lives we can no longer handle and bear. The picture we want to present to God, ourselves, and to the world is that "we are just fine — really!" But the truth for most of us *most* of the time, and for all of us at some time or other is that when we say we are "fine" it often really means we are,

> **F**razzled,
> **I**nsecure,
> **N**eurotic, and
> **E**motional.

Sooner or later we all have to admit the truth of the apostle Paul's great insight into human nature: we just can't hack it because the good that we would do, we can't; and the evil we don't want to do is exactly what we end up doing over and over again! (Romans 7:15-25). What scripture describes is true for every human experience from something supposedly as simple as eating right and getting enough exercise, to more complicated matters of interpersonal relationships and our central relationship with God.

Maybe you're like me: as a Lutheran-flavored Christian I may believe that I live by God's grace, but all too often I act, as one theologian said, "like a scout collecting merit badges." My days can quickly get filled up with long lists of duties and "oughts" and "have-to-dos" so that others — my wife, my children, the congregation I serve, even God — will love me more. Perhaps you, too, resemble that description?

But if we keep on with our own efforts at self-justification we will finally meet our own personal Waterloo of total defeat. If we say "no" to everything and everybody really important, including God, in order to get our "oughts" done, what we end up with is nothing and nobody. Then, as Paul describes in Romans, chapter seven, we become prisoners of despair, exhausted and overloaded.

Who can save us from this hopeless situation? It is only Jesus, the one who offers the "great invitation" in Matthew, chapter eleven. Our only option is surrender; to give it all up to Jesus; to lay all of our burdens down at the foot of his cross and admit that we can't handle life on our own. When we come to Jesus, take his yoke upon us and find rest, then we become prisoners of hope instead of prisoners of despair.

That hope is offered not to those who believe themselves to be super-saints, but, according to Matthew 11:25, to those who are ordinary people, as the phrase "little ones" can be translated. While in the modern business world insider trading information is usually only available to the bigwigs of a company that is not the case in the kingdom of God. According to Jesus, God holds nothing back. When it comes to our salvation God takes no chances with our future. Instead, God in Christ puts God's own self at risk on the cross, on our behalf, so that we no longer have to be at risk. Intimate insider knowledge of the Father is open to the rank and file — to all the "little ones," to you and to me — through faith in Jesus.

Therefore, because we know the heart of the Father we can accept Jesus' gracious invitation. What a relief to finally give in and surrender to the love of God and lay all the weariness and burdens down and then take up Jesus' yoke of discipleship. That's what Paul discovered; that's what Luther and all the great reformers of the church through history discovered. All who come to Jesus find what they really need — the rest of service to God and others.

Yes, I said the *rest* of *service*! Jesus says, "Take my yoke upon you... and you will find rest for your souls." The paradoxical combination of yoke and rest again shows that life in the kingdom is not a matter of anything goes, which leads to anarchy. The yoke here is a metaphor for discipleship. A yoke is a means of disciplining and organizing the strength of oxen for a purpose. What Jesus is talking about in these verses is the yoke of servant discipleship. Oftentimes the best kind of therapy for someone who is overwhelmed with life is for that person to focus instead on the needs of others. That is what God in Christ calls us to.

This yoke of service is easy because it is not a burden of compulsion, but a response of thanksgiving, love, and joy at God's grace that takes away the heaviness of guilt and shame through the forgiveness of sins. This yoke of service is light because it is the burden of freedom. The burden of freedom, as we are reminded on this Sunday closest to the July Fourth holiday, is so precious that it is worth dying for so that others may have it as well.

The yoke of discipleship is easy, not because all of the hard things of life will automatically disappear as soon as we believe in Jesus, but because we are yoked together with other disciples. We don't have to carry it on our own. Heather, our river rafting guide, was wrong and her mother was right:

we need the body of Christ. We need one another. We're in this thing together. Jesus sends his disciples out, not on their own, but together, two by two. We are to bear one another's burdens. Where two or three are gathered in Jesus' name, there — and only there — does he promise his freeing and comforting presence.

So Jesus wants the yoke — not the cruel joke of an overburdened life — to be on us. This invitation is not burdensome; it is not heavy. It moves us from being prisoners of despair to prisoners of hope. It makes it possible for us to have our strength renewed through the refreshing rest of service to God and others in Jesus' name.

Don't put off your response to Jesus' gracious invitation any longer. Come to him, all you who are weary and carrying heavy burdens, and he will give you rest. Take his yoke of discipleship upon you and learn from him; for he is gentle and humble of heart, and you will find rest for your souls. For his yoke is easy, and his burden is light.

So come to Jesus! Come, today! Come, right now! Come! Amen.

Proper 10 / Pentecost 6 / Ordinary Time 15
Matthew 13:1-9, 18-23

Lord, Let My Heart Be Good Soil

The song "Lord, Let My Heart Be Good Soil"[1] by Handt Hanson, is a beautiful piece that suggests a deep sense of longing for something important. The melody, tone, and words all come together perfectly as an interpretation of the gospel reading for today. While it is tempting to want to move on immediately to what a story like the parable of the sower *means* that reaction is usually an attempt to distance ourselves from the personal impact of the story. The story is safer if we can intellectualize it and then conveniently rationalize it away and not have to deal with the emotions stirred up by the message.

For example, we all know that a love letter is not meant to be analyzed — nothing can kill off a declaration of love faster than over-analysis. No, a love letter simply calls for a response on the part of the loved one.

In a similar way, the song "Lord, Let My Heart Be Good Soil" reminds us that the proper reaction to Jesus' parables is not analysis but a response of commitment to and longing for the reign of the love of God in our world and lives. That love for which we long is the source of our sense of belonging and feeling at home with God.

After living in any community for a length of time, and learning some of the history of the place, you eventually discover what the secret of truly belonging in that place is. In the community where we reside and where I minister, Bluffton, Ohio, my wife and I learned that the secret to truly belonging was that you, or a family member, must have worked at some time for one particular corporation in town or for the local family-owned greenhouse. So, when both of our daughters began working at the greenhouse (owned by members of our congregation), we knew that we had finally really arrived and had become part of the community!

At the greenhouse, our daughters assisted the owners with the strenuous yet delicate work of tending for thousands of plants and trees, helping them to grow and develop to their full potential so that those plants and trees could provide beauty, shade, and fruit for others. What we get to do as fellow members of the Body of Christ — the church — is similar to that. While God is the sower who sows the seed and gives the growth, we have an important role to play as God's co-workers and gardener's assistants, helping others to grow in faith and discipleship.

So, our response, our theme song and prayer today is, "Lord, let our hearts be good soil!" That is our prayer, desire, and hope for all who are baptized into the kingdom of God's love. We pray that the heart of each child or adult brought to the font would be good soil for the promises of God planted in each one, so that the work of God begun at baptism would bear fruit all through each life and to eternity.

That is our prayer for *all* of our children, for our youth, and for every face we see here this morning, as well as for those who should be here but aren't for whatever reason. But we know, if we pray that others' hearts would be good soil, then we are asking God to begin with us and show us how to help that happen. We have a role in preparing the soil of every person brought to the waters of baptism as parents, sponsors, and witnesses; we are all our brothers' and sisters' keepers, concerned for them and their growth in following Jesus and the ways of God's kingdom.

But the prayer of longing is also for us, personally: "Lord, let *my* heart be good soil!" We pray that God would work the soil of our hearts and of our lives. Here we see the wisdom of what Martin Luther and other reformers rediscovered nearly 500 years ago: becoming a Christian is not a one-time event, but a life of daily conversion, growth, nurture, care, and vigilance. The discipline of the faith practices — like prayer, study, worship, witness, encouragement, serving, and giving — those practices are the means by which God's Spirit works the soil of our hearts and lives.

Our hearts and lives needs to be worked because our sinful nature — the old Adam and Eve in us — though drowned in the waters of baptism, keeps floating back up to the surface and has to be drowned again through daily repentance. In the language of today's gospel reading, the old Adam and Eve are like weeds that keep coming up — they have to be plucked out, dug up, and thrown away. The more you keep at this spiritual weeding, the easier it becomes, but if you let it go for too long, the weeds of our sin can take over, and, just like a neglected garden, it can be overwhelming, depressing, just too much to handle. That's where the faith practices of daily prayer, study, worship, witness, encouragement, serving, giving, and the like come in.

God's Spirit, working through the faith practices, makes it possible for us to put it all together: to receive and understand and respond to the seed of God's good news planted in our hearts. Like a flower turning toward the sun, and leaves reaching up and out, soaking up the rain, prayer and praise open us up to God's agenda and God's blessings. Through prayer and praise we turn away from the cares, worries, agenda, and priorities of self and the world and turn back to God and the kingdom's ways each day.

Through daily digging into the Bible, God's word breaks up the hard soil of our hearts. Then the power of forgiveness can remove the rocks of anger, jealousy, prejudice, and fear that lie just beneath the surface, making it difficult for God's love to take root in our lives and thrive and bear fruit. A plant that does not bear fruit has no future. In the same way, the faith we have must be shared, it must be passed on. This is our purpose: to bear fruit for God by witnessing or testifying to what God has done for us in the death and resurrection of Christ Jesus. That witness, then, will show itself, not in words of criticism, judgment, anger, and fear, but in words of challenging encouragement and loving acts of sacrificial serving and giving.

Jesus' parable of the seeds, then, is a gracious invitation from God to grow into all that God wants us to be. Don't over-analyze the invitation. The proper response is one of active commitment to and longing for the reign of the love of God in our world and in our lives.

God promises to do his part. His word does not go out empty, but accomplishes God's purposes and succeeds in that for which God sent it (Isaiah 55:11). The seed that falls on good soil, prepared by our doing of the faith practices will produce an amazing harvest for God.

"Lord, let *our* hearts be good soil!" That is my prayer for each of you. Please, let that be your prayer for me and for one another. And let's make that our daily prayer, starting right now for all of our young ones, Lord, let their hearts be good soil! Then, let's rejoice at what God will do in their hearts and in ours, in their lives and in ours, because the power of God at work within us is able to accomplish far more than all we can ask or imagine (Ephesians 3:20). The One who has called us to himself is faithful, and he will do it (1 Thessalonians 5:24).

Amen.

---

1. "Lord, Let My Heart Be Good Soil," text and music by Handt Hanson. Copyright 1985 Prince of Peace Publishing. Changing Church, Inc.

Proper 11 / Pentecost 7 / Ordinary Time 16
Matthew 13:24-30, 36-43

Dealing with T-A-R-E-ists

This is a hard text for me because I am a typical first child in many respects. You other first children may recognize yourselves in some of what I'm about to say. As a first child I want everything to be black and white, and so, when things go wrong, I become a problem solver who wants to make it all right again. But that doesn't always work out, as I discovered the year I was eight. Just before Christmas that year I decided I needed to "fix" the family Christmas tree decorations and, in the process of straightening the star on the top of the tree, pulled the whole thing over on top of me!

My desire to immediately want to make things right doesn't go over too well in our relationship to our grown-up daughters, either. My wife Debbie and I can't fix things for them anymore; we can't kiss the scraped knee and make it all better. All we can do now is just listen and wait; be patient and trust in the wisdom we tried to instill in them as we raised them as children of God and followers of Jesus Christ. We have to trust in the good seed sown by God's Spirit in their hearts. We have to trust in the fruit and the harvest that God — not we — will make in their lives.

Patient trust in God is one of the things the parable in the gospel reading is all about. The weeds spoken of here in the text were translated as "tares" in the old KJV. Tares were a ryegrass, a poisonous plant that was widespread in ancient Palestine. In its immature stages it looked almost identical to a young wheat plant. The two could only be easily distinguished when the plants reached the seed-bearing stage — as the Bible says, "you will know them by their fruit."

The servants of the master farmer, in the parable told by Jesus, were shocked to find tares growing in the field sown with the master's good seed. They must have been first-children because in the face of this abomination caused, we are told (by the enemy of the master) the servants want to immediately fix the problem by tearing out the weeds and make things right again. But the master says, "No, wait, be patient; let's not cause any collateral damage; it will all get sorted out at the harvest."

Jesus, in the words of the master, is teaching us the reality we all experience: weeds or tares, both literally and spiritually, are a post-Eden fact of life in the world, the church, and in our lives. Weeds or tares happen, so we have to learn to deal with the TARE-ists — that's T-A-R-E-ists in a Christ-like way without becoming TEAR-orists — that's T-E-A-R-orists — ourselves.

The kingdom of God on earth is a messy, mixed field where good and bad stuff and people are so intermingled that it's not safe or good for us to try to separate them with our own limited wisdom and vision; a vision that only sees through a mirror dimly in this life. We don't like the messy ambiguity of who's in or out, so we want to draw a line in the sand. The problem with drawing lines in the sand, or in immediately trying to tear out the tares, is that by drawing that line we may be actually drawing ourselves outside of God's gracious heart, or in trying to tear out the T-A-R-E-ists — we may actually be uprooting ourselves!

As someone once humorously said, "I am certain there will be three surprises in heaven: I will see some people there I never expected to see; there will be a number of people missing whom I expected to see there; and there will be others who will be surprised to see me there!"

In other words, the bad news/good news of the reign of God is that God started down the road of freedom and love a long time ago, and he will not turn back from that path. Freedom, as we learn every day in the flawed workings of American democracy, for example, is a messy business. It takes patience and trust. We see the same in God's running of the world. God takes the risk of not being too hasty with the weeding process. God's justice seems to take a long time because God is gracious and merciful, slow to anger, and abounding in steadfast love, as Psalm 86:15 reminds us.

The truth of the matter, though, is that God's patient mercy drives us crazy at times — except that is, when we need and want him to be patient with us and our sins! The truth Jesus reveals in this parable is hard for us to accept because he's telling us something we really don't want to hear. When we encounter what we see as evil our immediate reaction is to want to go on a hunt-and-destroy mission. Our battle cry becomes, "Don't just stand there — do something!"

But that's not what Jesus says to us in this parable. In fact, the parable turns our conventional wisdom on its head when Jesus has the landowner say in effect, "Don't just do something, stand there!" Jesus is teaching us the important lesson that we are called as his disciples not just to be against things, but instead to be for the good that God will cause to prosper and grow as we wait with the trusting patience of mercy.

It is all about patience: not roll over and play dead patience, not head in the sand patience, but active patience that concentrates on the good, not on the bad. This active patience trusts that the ultimate victory is God's, and that the power of God's antidote of the good news in Christ Jesus is far stronger than the poison of the tares, the bad seed. In short, how we live among the weeds, among the tares, is vital. It is vital that we live as patient, forgiving disciples because, while weeds always remain weeds, and wheat always remains wheat in the natural world, in God's spiritual agriculture God never writes anyone off before death. People can change under the power of God's mercy, as the example of the repentant thief on the cross shows and as we know from personal experience.

So the default setting for us is not to be T-E-A-R-orists, but to deal with T-A-R-E-ists patiently with forgiveness. Some biblical scholars have pointed out the perhaps intentional linguistic hint at the connection to forgiveness in verse 30. When the landowner tells his servants to allow the wheat and the tares to grow up together, the original Greek for "allow" is the same word used for "forgive" in Matthew's version of the Lord's Prayer, to forgive as we have been forgiven. To not practice forgiveness is to run the risk of becoming just like the evil we are trying to uproot and remove.

A proverb says, "Choose your enemies carefully, because you become like them."[1] How true! It is very easy to become intolerant with intolerant people, or angry at people who are angry at us, or bigoted toward bigoted people. By seeking to destroy our enemies, we usually condemn ourselves because we have become just like them, as another proverb says, "Be careful, lest in fighting the dragon, you become the dragon."

Haven't we seen that danger in some of the responses by the United States to September 11, 2001? In our understandable desire to root out and destroy terrorists, we have been tempted to violate our own principles and constitution with the use of surrogates, torture, and imprisonment without trial of our enemies, and questionable surveillance techniques at home. And then, as we have also seen in both Iraq and Afghanistan — crusades, even those done with the best of intentions and out of the highest motives — almost always result in collateral damage, the loss of innocent lives caught in the crossfire of our passion, whether it be for democracy and freedom, or even for the truth of the gospel and pure theology.

The story is told that in one of the first crusades, knights from Western Europe attacked an Arab town on their way to the holy land and killed everyone in sight. It was not until later, when they turned the bodies over, that they found crosses around most of their victims' necks. It had never occurred to them that Christians came in brown skin as well as in white.[2]

The fact is, we often can't tell the wheat from the weeds, because they are so often intertwined. We even know that to be true at the personal level because in this life all of us who are followers of Jesus Christ are still saints and sinners at the same time. The struggle with the presence of sin in our lives continues even as we pray to be fruitful for God and the kingdom.

Jesus makes clear in the parable that we simply cannot be certain who is "in" or who is "out," and thank God it is not up to us to decide! We can leave the weeding to the angels on the last day, and get on with the mission Jesus has given us — proclaiming the good news of the kingdom of God. We do not have to defend God. As someone wisely said, "You defend God like you defend a lion — you get out of his way."[3]

The landowner in the parable did not panic at the actions of his enemy because he knew he would make it all right in the harvest, reaping the good and destroying the bad. In the meantime, the landowner was more interested in seeing things grow than he was in having a pure and tidy field. Jesus is saying to us here that we can relax. We don't have to be in the judging business or in the business of destroying that which works against God. The owner of the "farm," God himself, will make it all come out right in the end, as the apostle Paul reminds us in Romans, chapter 8, "we know that all things work together for good for those who love God, who are called according to his purpose." We can trust in that promise because in the cross and the resurrection Jesus Christ died and lived out the meaning of this parable. Hanging on the cross, he did not seek to destroy his enemies who sowed the lethal seeds of death that choked out his life. Instead, he forgave them, trusted in his Father's will to sort it out in the end, and while he was hanging there he focused on the good wheat around him and drew the thief on the cross into the harvest of paradise.

The power of the resurrection proves the truth of the parable of the wheat and weeds. Therefore we can recommit ourselves to leaving the weeds to God while, with all our hearts and souls, we patiently work at nurturing the growth of the wheat God has sown in us, around us, and among us, while we wait for the harvest with joy!

Amen.

Some concepts adapted from:
The Lectionary Gospel: Matthew 13:24-30, 36-43, by Scott Hoezee, 2015
http://cep.calvinseminary.edu/sermon-starters/proper-11a/?type=the_lectionary_gospel
1. The original full quote is from Friedrich Nietzsche, *Beyond Good and Evil, Aphorism 146.*
2. I was not able to find an original source for this "crusade" story. It has been widely quoted in many sermons found online.
3. The exact source of the quote is unknown. Augustine of Hippo said something similar about the Word of God, and Charles Spurgeon used similar wording a number of times in sermons. See, http://www.allaboutgod.net/profiles/blogs/the-word-of-god-is-like-a, posted by Yoel Charan, 2009, accessed on May 15, 2015

Proper 12 / Pentecost 8 / Ordinary Time 17
Matthew 13:31-33, 44-52

A Working God

As I originally prepared this sermon the news was breaking about the tragedy in Charleston, South Carolina in 2015, with the Honorable Reverend Pinckney and eight of his parishioners gunned down in the historic black Emmanuel A.M.E. church. But this tragic act couldn't be conveniently blamed on Islamic extremists. No! This time the perpetrator in custody had the blasphemous audacity to pretend to be one of us and claim the name of Christ as his Lord, and, in fact, was a member of a congregation of my own church denomination!

How do we come to terms with tragedies like that and these words of the apostle Paul in Romans 8: "We know that all things work together for good [or as it can be translated, we know that in all things God works together for good] for those who love God, who are called according to his purpose"?

Out of our silence, struck dumb by the evil at work around us and in us, the Spirit of God helps us in our weakness and confusion and terror, speaking to us and for us and through us to others with sighs too deep for words, pointing us to Jesus Christ.

Our Lord and Savior was not a stranger to hardship and tragedy. In the context surrounding the parables of Jesus in Matthew 13, we are told, first, of the gathering opposition to Jesus, including that of his own family. As a former missionary I have heard stories from other missionaries whose call to serve overseas was misunderstood and opposed by family members, as Jesus' ministry was by his relatives according to Matthew 12. Then, immediately after chapter 13, we are informed of the senseless beheading of Jesus' cousin, John the Baptizer by Herod. John's fate calls to mind that of those hostages executed in our time by the terrorist group ISIS.

In a world of such barbarity and ambiguity about the existence or even presence of God in human affairs, we dare to proclaim that God is present and at work in the matters of this life. Even more radical and audacious, we believe that God can and does work in and through even the worst tragedies of this life. That is what the cross and the resurrection means. We're not just talking about dry doctrines we learned back in catechism class, folks. It is in the face of tragedies that our faith is shown to be most real and authentic. It was in the face of the tragedy of the cross that God's love burst on the scene of the human predicament in all of its freeing power. It is that love which makes God's claim on our lives for his kingdom.

The kingdom of God's love is at work in our messed up lives and world. God at work: this is what the parables in Matthew, chapter thirteen are about. The kingdom of God, therefore, is more of a verb than a noun; it is an action, not an object — the reign or the rule of God over our lives and the world. So, in the parables, Jesus isn't really comparing the kingdom to five things, but rather to five actions. Jesus doesn't say the kingdom of heaven is *like* a pearl, but that it's like a merchant *in search* of pearls. The kingdom is like a mustard seed that someone *took* and *sowed* in a field, and which then *grew*; like yeast that a woman *took* and *mixed* and then *leavened*; like a treasure that someone *found* and *hid*; like a net that was *thrown* and then *caught* things. All of those *things* — mustard seed, yeast, a net, a treasure, a pearl — all are useless if they are not put to work and used in some way. Likewise, the kingdom of God is not some lifeless, inanimate object that we can look at, appreciate, and study; it is the very life and purpose of God put into action for us and in us for God and for others.

God is at work, not just in some exotic, far-off place that requires a special map. The "X" of the cross of Christ marks the spot right here, right now in the very ordinariness of our lives and places and activities that are all-too-often touched by the tragedies of life. This is where God is at work.

God works, and when God works the end product is not junk! Being caught up in the working of God's Kingdom is like finding a hidden treasure; its value, like that of a pearl of great price, is more precious than all that we have. God can make a masterpiece out of the messiness of our lives. God can transpose our disharmony into a symphony of praise. God can take the setbacks and losses and even the tragedies in our lives and turn them into great victories because in Christ "we are more than conquerors through him who loved us" (Romans 8:37).

We are not in denial here. Not everything that happens to us in this life is good. Evil and sin are real. As the parable of the net teaches with the separation of the good and bad fish, there are and will be real dire consequences to our rejection of God's gracious reign. But what scripture proclaims and we believe is that the final word God desires to speak over us is not rejection. God's desire is that none should perish, but that all should come to repentance through faith in Jesus Christ. In Christ we know that God is for us, not against us; there is now no condemnation for those who are in Christ Jesus, and nothing in all of creation — not any natural or human-caused disaster; no crazed fanatic in Charleston or anywhere else — can separate us from the love of God in Christ Jesus (2 Peter 3:9; Romans 8:31-39).

God is at work, and though what God does in and through us and for us may at first appear to be insignificant, like a tiny mustard seed, God's reign grows in us so that our lives and our community of faith can be places of refuge and nurture for others. God's work at times is nearly invisible but, like leaven, is powerful in its effects, changing us from the inside out to become the people God wants us to be. The reign of God's love at work in our lives is so precious that, like a pearl of great price, we will seek it out, giving up the precious commodity of our time in order to be where God's Spirit promises to be present: in prayer and praise and study of God's word with other followers of Jesus.

Therefore, as God's workmanship, as God's masterpieces, created for good works, we are signs of the kingdom of God in action. We have the great responsibility, privilege, and joy of reaching out to all those who are touched by the tragedies of life. The message we have to share is very straightforward: God's love in Christ Jesus is still working for good in this world!

Amen to that!

Other CSS Titles by R. Kevin Mohr

Holy Saturday
An Easter Chancel Drama in Three Acts
0788026739
5.5 x 8.5
32 pages

Sermons on the First Readings
Series III, Cycle C
Pentecost 3: "Restoring God's Activity"
Derl G. Keefer, David J. Kalas, Stephen P. McCutchan, Chrysanne Timm, R. Kevin Mohr
0788026194
5.5x8.5
426 pages

www.ingramcontent.com/pod-product-compliance
Lightning Source LLC
Chambersburg PA
CBHW071800040426
42446CB00012B/2650